797,885 Books

are available to read at

www.ForgottenBooks.com

Forgotten Books' App
Available for mobile, tablet & eReader

ISBN 978-1-332-86387-7
PIBN 10269C14

This book is a reproduction of an important historical work. Forgotten Books uses
state-of-the-art technology to digitally reconstruct the work, preserving the original format
whilst repairing imperfections present in the aged copy. In rare cases, an imperfection in
the original, such as a blemish or missing page, may be replicated in our edition. We do,
however, repair the vast majority of imperfections successfully; any imperfections that
remain are intentionally left to preserve the state of such historical works.

Forgotten Books is a registered trademark of FB &c Ltd.
Copyright © 2015 FB &c Ltd.
FB &c Ltd, Dalton House, 60 Windsor Avenue, London, SW19 2RR.
Company number 08720141. Registered in England and Wales.

For support please visit www.forgottenbooks.com

1 MONTH OF FREE READING

at
www.ForgottenBooks.com

By purchasing this book you are eligible for one month membership to ForgottenBooks.com, giving you unlimited access to our entire collection of over 700,000 titles via our web site and mobile apps.

To claim your free month visit:
www.forgottenbooks.com/free269014

* Offer is valid for 45 days from date of purchase. Terms and conditions apply.

English
Français
Deutsche
Italiano
Español
Português

www.forgottenbooks.com

Mythology Photography **Fiction**
Fishing Christianity **Art** Cooking
Essays Buddhism Freemasonry
Medicine **Biology** Music **Ancient
Egypt** Evolution Carpentry Physics
Dance Geology **Mathematics** Fitness
Shakespeare **Folklore** Yoga Marketing
Confidence Immortality Biographies
Poetry **Psychology** Witchcraft
Electronics Chemistry History **Law**
Accounting **Philosophy** Anthropology
Alchemy Drama Quantum Mechanics
Atheism Sexual Health **Ancient History**
Entrepreneurship Languages Sport
Paleontology Needlework Islam
Metaphysics Investment Archaeology
Parenting Statistics Criminology
Motivational

THE GUILFORD FAMILY

IN AMERICA

Pedigrees and Genealogical Notes of the Guilford and allied Families

---

ARRANGED FOR THE CHILDREN OF NATHAN AND
MARY WALLACE GUILFORD, OF
YONKERS, N. Y.

By their Father

Allen County Public Library
Ft. Wayne, Indiana

THAT my children may know something of the stock from which they spring, I have gleaned here and there, from my parents and kinsfolk, and from the early records and histories of New England towns and parishes, such scraps and threads of family history as I could find, and have woven them into the following sketch. Imperfect as it is, it will show their descent from a line of honorable and patriotic ancestors, all of Anglo-Saxon blood on their father's side, with an admixture of a strain of Hollander stock in their mother's ancestry.

Only 50 copies of this book have been printed.

This copy is No. 5

THE NAME OF GUILFORD.

Guilford is an ancient and historic English name. The town of Guilford, in Surrey, is mentioned in the will of Alfred the Great. Kent adjoins Surrey; and when Shakespeare says

"In Kent, my liege, the Guilfords are in arms"
(Richard III., Act IV., Sc. 4),

he indicates the power and influence of that family in the 15th century. In fact, Sir Richard Guylforde, Knight, of Hempsted in Kent, was an eminent personage of ancient family who took the field for the Duke of Richmond against Richard III., and was rewarded by many royal grants from the Duke after he became King Henry VII. He was High Sheriff of Kent, Comptroller of the royal household, lord of several manors and Knight of the Garter; his garter-plate may still be seen in St. George's Chapel.

The interesting story of his pilgrimage to the holy land in 1506, quaintly told by his chaplain, is in the British Museum; and I have a copy of its reprint by the Camden Society, which also shows the family pedigree back to the 12th century, in which the name is variously spelt Guldeford, Guildeford, Guildford or Guilford, according to individual taste, or perhaps through indifference to what was regarded as a trifling matter. Such variations are not unusual in the spelling of proper names, or, in fact, of any words. In the course of centuries great changes have been made in orthography ; in earlier times but little importance was attached to it, even among the better educated.

Such changes are still constantly going on. When in London in 1890 I passed through a street bearing our name, which was written "Guilford" on some of the street corners and "Guildford" on others. In the earlier town records of New England, the name is frequently spelled "Gilford," and sometimes "Gillfoord"— such variations in spelling family names being common during the period of early settlement of the country, owing to the varying orthography used by town clerks and other recorders.

The name also belongs to the North Family, the title of Earl of Guilford having been in 1683 conferred by Charles II. on Francis North, Lord Keeper of the Great Seal, who transmitted it to his descendant of revolutionary fame. But our right to the name is older than theirs ; for before they assumed it our American born ancestor, Paul Guilford, of Hingham, was fighting King Philip's Indians in defense of his New England home.

As to the etymology of the name : surnames, as family names, were unknown before the 11th century and were not in common use until the 14th. They usually designated estate, place of residence, occupation, or perhaps had reference to some personal trait. Guild or Gild, in Anglo-Saxon, means a payment. Ford, in Anglo-Saxon, means a passage, especially through a river. We may fancy, if we please, that our Anglo-Saxon ancestors levied tolls at the fords, and that the name was thence derived.

But while we have inherited from English forefathers this old and historic name, we do not know that the first immigrants to America who bore it were descendants from the illustrious Knights of Hempsted; nor from what part of England they came; nor the motive which impelled them to cross the Atlantic to seek their fortunes in the New World, and encounter the perils and hardships which awaited the pioneer settlers of New England.

There is, however, a circumstance which, if it does not show a connection between us and the Guilfords of Kent, is at least worth recording as an interesting coincidence; and that is our supposed relationship to the Dudley family of New England, which is descended from the Dudleys of Old England, who were closely related to the Guilfords of Kent.

Their immigrant ancestor, Thomas Dudley, came from England in 1630, bearing the King's Commission as Deputy Governor of Massachusetts colony. He was son of Captain Roger Dudley, a "captain in the wars" in the reign of Elizabeth, and was descended from the Barons of Dudley,* of whom John Dudley, Duke of Northumberland and Earl of Warwick, married Jane Guilford, granddaughter of Sir Richard Guylforde, of the "Pylgrymage." She was the mother of Guilford Dudley, who married Lady Jane Grey, and of Robert Dudley, Earl of Leicester, the favorite of Queen Elizabeth, and was grandmother of Sir Philip Sidney. Through her marriage (temp. Henry VIII.) the Guilford and Dudley families

* N. E. Hist. and Gen. Reg. x, 133.

were allied, and among their descendants the name of "Guilford Dudley" has reappeared through successive generations.

According to a family tradition we are related to the New England Dudleys, but in what manner does not appear. There seems to be no record of their intermarriage on this side of the ocean. My uncle Asa Guilford used to say they were akin; he probably heard so from his father or grandfather.

William Dudley, grandson of Governor Thomas, was one of the twenty-two original grantees of the town of Leicester, part of which afterwards formed the town of Spencer. In 1730 this tract was apportioned among the several grantees, who were required by the terms of the grant to procure actual settlers upon the land assigned to them. The one who settled upon Dudley's land was my great-grandfather, John Guilford. It seems probable that some relation existed between them.

THE GUILFORD FAMILY IN AMERICA.

❧ ❧ ❧

The record in my father's old family Bible says that we are descended from an ancestor who emigrated from England to Scituate, Massachusetts, and who settled at Hingham, about ten miles from Scituate. Hingham was settled about 1634; its early town and parish records are incomplete, but they show the death of

JOHN GUILFORD September 26th, 1660. How long he had been a resident of Hingham is not known, but he must have lived there at least ten years, for he married there, and the births of his three children are recorded, the eldest in 1651. We also find that MARY GUILFORD, widow, died at Hingham May 7th, 1660. She was probably John's mother, and the record tends to confirm the truth of a family tradition which relates that our ancestor first went from England to Virginia with his family, but returned thence to England where he died, and that the widow, with her son or sons, then emigrated to New England. John Guilford married, about 1650, Susanna Norton, only child of William and Ann Norton, of Hingham. Their children were:

1. Susanna, born in Hingham November 2d, 1651, who on October 15, 1672, married Thomas Jewell, also a native of Hingham. Lincoln's History of Hingham records the interesting fact that their seats in church were directly opposite each other. He was son of Thomas Jewell, of Kingston-upon-Thames, England, who emigrated on the "Planter" in April, 1635.

2. Paul.

3. Priscilla, born April 22d, 1660, who died in infancy.

PAUL GUILFORD, only son of John, was born in Hingham August 14th, 1653, and married Susanna Pullen February 20th, 1677. They had four children, born in Hingham ·

1. Mary, June 20th, 1679, who married Thomas Curtice, of Scituate.
2. Elizabeth, February 9th, 1683.
3. Hester, and
4. William.

Paul was a soldier in Joshua Hobart's company, in Captain Samuel Wardsworth's company, and also in Captain John Holbrook's company in King Philip's Indian War in 1675–6.* He was also a soldier in King William's War between the New England Colonies and the Canadian French with their Indian allies, and he perished, aged 37 years, in the unfortunate Canada expedition in 1690, under the command of Sir William Phipps.† His wife Susanna also died in 1690, April 8th.

The records of "Suffolk County Deeds" show that Paul acquired by purchase other lands besides those inherited from his grandfather, and that they were afterwards possessed by his children. He is also recorded as one of the proprietors of lands in Maine, though he seems to have never gone there himself.

WILLIAM GUILFORD, only son of Paul, was born in Hingham, June, 1689, and was left an orphan the following year. His nearest relative, besides his young sisters, was his aunt, Mrs. Jewell, who lived at Amesbury, many miles distant. In an instrument under the hand of Paul Guilford, bearing date July 5th, 1690, and mentioned in

---

* Bodge's Soldiers of King Philip's War. ·
† Hist. Hingham i. 237; ii. 268.

the records of Suffolk County,* certain lands were set apart for the use and bringing up of his son William, who seems to have been taken charge of by a Scituate family, and to have made his home in that place. Perhaps it was from this circumstance that my father derived the belief that our first ancestor settled in Scituate. As late as in 1724 William is recorded as a resident of Scituate, and as selling a part of his Hingham land. He afterwards removed to Leicester, Mass., where he settled near "Shaw's Pond." There were but few inhabitants in Leicester at this time, owing to the hostility of the Indians. William passed the remainder of his days there, and his grave is under the site of the old church at Leicester. After his death his widow and son went back to Hingham to recover some lands formerly owned by him, but their claim was contested and they did not succeed. William had two children, besides a daughter, who died in infancy ·

1. John.
2. William. 7th Great Grandfather

JOHN GUILFORD, son of William, was born in 1720, lived for some years in Leicester and removed to Spencer, Mass., of which he was one of the first settlers, and in which place he died in 1815, aged 95, and was buried in the old churchyard there. He was a soldier in the old French war, was tall, of large frame, and vigorous up to the time of his death. He married in 1750 Susanna Whitney, of Shrewsbury, Mass. The children of John and Susanna were:

1. John (1752–1828), a Harvard student and a revolutionary soldier, who was in Arnold's expedition against Quebec, undertaken eighty-six years after the similar attempt in which his great-grandfather Paul perished. He married Sarah Flagg May 8th, 1793.

* Deeds, Vol. xxi, p. 338.

2. Asa (1755–1775), a Harvard student and revolutionary soldier.

3. Samuel (1757 ——), a revolutionary soldier and pensioner, who married a Miss Cranson.

4. Jonas.

5. William (1761–1807), a farmer, whose first wife was a widow (Bemis) Green, and whose second wife was —— Boyden.

6. Lucy, who married Nathan Bemis.

7. Nathan, who died in infancy.

The old family homestead in Spencer, built about 1804, stood until 1894, when it was demolished in order to build a new house upon the same foundation. All the wood in it was cut upon the home farm. It had six fire-places and a brick oven. The chimney was about twelve feet square at the base, and contained almost bricks enough to build a modern house. (See frontispiece.)

JONAS GUILFORD, fourth son of John, was born in Spencer, August 25th, 1759, and died in 1809. He was but a school-boy when the Revolutionary war broke out, and his three elder brothers, aged 18, 20 and 23 years, took up arms in the cause of the Colonies. He entered upon the study of medicine, and on the declaration of peace in 1783, he married Lydia Hobbs, of Brookfield, Mass. (born 1760, died 1848). In personal appearance he resembled his father, but was of somewhat lesser stature. He was a practising physician in Spencer for twenty-six years. His children were:

1. Betsey (1784-1855), married Nathaniel Bemis.

2. Nathan.

3. Jonas (1788-1866), who studied medicine with Dr. Babbit, of Brookfield, and was a practising physician in Spencer for half a century. He was a very large man, and was much respected both as a man and a physician. He married Persis Bemis and had six daughters, two of whom, Maria and Jane are, I believe, still living in Spencer, unmarried. His only grandchild, Asa Jones, was living in Colorado a few years ago, an invalid.

4. Charles (1791-1871), was a soldier in the war of 1812. His son, Charles C., was a well-known school teacher in Cincinnati for many years, and now lives in Iowa. His daughter, Harriet, married —— Marvin, also a school teacher of Cincinnati.

5. John (1793-1832), was also a soldier in the war of 1812, and was at the battle of Plattsburg. He married Dolly Sumner, and their only son settled as a farmer on Rock River, Illinois.

6. Lydia (1795-1865), unmarried.

7. Sally (1797-1845), married Otis Grout : had four children.

8. George (1799-1868), married Jane Ely: had one son, George, Jr., now living in Cincinnati, O.

9. Asa (1802-1891), married Mary Adams (1804-1884), of Brookfield, Mass. Their son Jonas was born in Spencer, Mass., September 17th, 1839, married September 30th, 1869, Helen Morrill, of Danville, Vermont (born October, 9th, 1841); removed to Minneapolis, Minn., May, 1867; was graduated from Amherst College; practises law in Minneapolis. His children are:

   (1) Harry Morrill, born March 25th, 1872, a student at the University of Minnesota ; (2) Harriet, born February 2d, 1874, a student at Carleton College, Northfield, Minn.; (3) Paul Willis, born January 15th, 1876, a student at the University of Minnesota.

NATHAN GUILFORD, eldest son of Jonas, was born in Spencer, July 19th, 1786. He was graduated at Yale in 1812, and after studying law, emigrated to Kentucky, where he practised in Alexandria, in partnership with Amos Kendall. In 1816 he settled in Cincinnati, Ohio, and was, until his death, one of its most prominent and esteemed citizens.

The early settlers of the "Northwestern Territory" (from the eastern part of which Ohio was formed) were mostly indifferent to the value of education; they allowed their children to grow up in ignorance, and so dreaded taxation that they bitterly opposed any plan of maintaining schools at public expense.

Nathan Guilford made the cause of education of the masses the first object of his life. He quit the practise of law and set about creating a public sentiment in favor of free education to all. At this task he labored for years, and in 1825, having been elected to the Senate on that issue, he introduced a bill which, after the strongest opposition, finally became a law. Its passage caused great excitement, and many believed that its enforcement would cause an insurrection. Popular prejudice was yet to be overcome, but this was done by degrees.

In 1828 he, with his brother George, opened a book and publishing house at No. 14 Lower Market Street, and afterwards removed to Main Street near the court-house, where they continued in business until about 1840. He established the "Cincinnati Daily Atlas" in 1843, and conducted it for several years. He was also interested in the Cincinnati Type Foundry, and afterwards opened the Ohio Type Foundry, which was not successful. In 1850, 1851 and 1852 he was Superintendent of the Cincinnati schools, and his daily visits to the recitation rooms made him well known to almost every child in the city. He died December 19th, 1854, and the newspapers of the time, as well as the testimonials from public bodies in my

NATHAN GUILFORD.

From a portrait painted about 1819.

private letter files, will give my children an idea of the respect and esteem with which he was regarded by the community.

These sentiments were fully justified, not only by his public services, but by his personal qualities. He was a man of elevated character, honorable, affectionate, amiable and purely unselfish. His fondness for study had given him an enormous fund of general information. He says in his diary that he required but three or four hours' sleep, and that he had learned the most of what he knew by studying when the rest of the household were asleep.

In personal appearance he was of fair complexion, blue eyes and light hair, which in his later years was white as snow and stood erect. He was over six feet tall and of large frame. Those of his brothers whom I have seen were also fair. His father and grandfather were large in stature and had reddish hair.

On October 29th, 1819, Nathan Guilford married ELIZA WHEELER FARNSWORTH. She was not only gifted with health, beauty and the warmest of hearts, but possessed marked strength of character, intelligence, self-reliance, untiring energy and an inexhaustible flow of high spirits which the physical infirmities brought by more than four score years in no way diminished, and which made her society sought and enjoyed by old and young. The children of Nathan and Eliza Guilford were :

1. Anna, born August 3, 1820, married Francis Donaldson, of Cincinnati. Their only child, Elizabeth, died young.

2. William, born July 10, 1823, died March 3, 1891; married Charlotte Kirby, of Cincinnati. Their children are:

(1) William, born 1848, married Mary Van Pelt; (2) Eugene Lemaire, born 1850; (3) Horace Hastings, born 1852, married Laura Stitt; (4) Charlotte B., born 1854, married Millard McCormick; (5) Henry H., born 1856; (6) Charles Wetmore, born 1858, married Elizabeth Dodd; (7) Edwin B., married Alberta Reynolds; (8) May, born 1867; (9) Nathan, born 1870.

3. Apolline, born March 10, 1825, married (1) George Donaldson, brother of Francis, named on page 15; (2) Clement Têtedoux, of Paris, France. The children of her second marriage are Clement, who married Lillian Elma Erd, and Marie, who married Frederick A. Schmidt. They live in Cincinnati.

4. Belle, born March 16, 1833, married (1) William S. Stewart, (2) Charles W. Barry.

5. Nathan.

I copy the following newspaper extracts from a number in my scrap book:

MARBLE IMMORTALITY.

Each State in the Union is authorized by a joint resolution of Congress to place in the statuary room in the Capitol at Washington statues or busts of two distinguished citizens of such State. For one of those Ohio has made provision—James A. Garfield having, by unanimous consent, been declared worthy of this great honor; an honor analogous to the *apotheosis* in ancient times bestowed upon men and women who had done great things for their country or for mankind, and who were, therefore, esteemed as worthy of having their names enrolled among the immortals. Ohio has yet another niche in this temple of fame. With whose statue shall that niche be filled? Who among the scores of heroes, statesmen, scholars and philanthropists, whose deeds, during three generations, have shed lustre upon the history of the State and nation, shall receive that high honor? * * * May there not be, outside of the turbulent arena of politics, outside of the factitious glamour of public office and official honors, a true, a genuine greatness worthy of commemoration in everlasting bronze or marble? Ignorance and degradation are twin brothers; an ignorant people can neither enjoy nor perpetuate the blessings of liberty.

NATHAN GUILFORD.

From a daguerreotype taken about 1850.

Such were the conceptions—such the teachings—of a citizen of Ohio seventy years ago. He was a school teacher. He had neither wealth nor influential friends—was rich only in his love of mankind, and happy in the assured friendship of the Great Master. His mission was a political one. He knew that he could accomplish nothing without the consent of the majority. He held private conferences with ministers of religion, with judges, magistrates, governors and law-makers. He traveled on foot, on horseback, on lumber wagons, on rafts and flatboats. He lectured in towns and villages and in log meeting-houses in the back settlements. He attended the meetings of the legislature. He was a lobbyist—a most persistent and importunate lobbyist—but not in the interest of himself or of any company, corporation or monopoly, but in the interest of the then present and all future generations. Finally, after repeated repulses and disappointments, his bill passed and received the signatures of the presiding officers of the two houses of the legislature.

His work was done—no: not done, for it will never be done so long as one generation of freemen succeeds another on this continent, and on all the continents and islands of the globe. That work is finished and begun again every year. It is not confined to Ohio; it pervades the continent. Thousands—aye, millions—who enjoy the inestimable benefits of his work have never heard his name pronounced. His statue ought to be set up in some conspicuous place in Cincinnati the city of his residence, and also on Capitol Square in Columbus, the scene of his labors year after year. * * *

The people of Ohio can in no way render greater honor to their fathers, themselves, their children and their State, than by filling Ohio's vacant niche at Washington with a statue or bust with this inscription: "NATHAN GUILFORD, Founder of the Common Schools of Ohio."—(*Ohio State Journal*, Jan. 16th, 1885.)

OUR EARLY BOOKSELLERS.

* * * About 1828 Nathan and George Guilford established a bookstore at No. 14 Lower Market Street. * * * The senior member of this firm was a distinguished scholar and lawyer who had been the law partner of Amos Kendall, in Georgetown, Ky., and afterward of J. W. Gazlay, in Cincinnati. He was a member of the Ohio Legislature, where he was the leading advocate of the common

school system, and did more than any other member to secure its adoption, for at that period it was far from being popular. Most of our old citizens are well aware of his meritorious efforts in the successful establishment of the system, and know that he may with justice be styled its "father." He subsequently engaged very successfully in the Cincinnati Type Foundry, to which he gave his personal supervision and care. For his able and successful advocacy of our school system he deserves a monument to his memory from the State society. This eminent and honored citizen died in 1854 amid the benedictions of our people, and especially the younger portion of them, who were largely benefited by his labors in the cause of education.—(*Cincinnati Gazette*, June 12th, 1880.)

※ ※ ※

The "Daily Atlas" was established in the autumn of 1843 by Nathan Guilford, who had long been known as one of the most prominent citizens of Cincinnati. Owing to his leadership in the Ohio Legislature in 1824, in establishing the common school system of the State, he was prominently known as the "Father of the Common Schools." He was a man of the most decided political convictions of the ultra Whig school, and was in declining years—over sixty—when he commenced his career as a journalist. The undertaking was much against the opposition of his family and advice of his true friends. They predicted that at his time of life he would be certain to fail in attempting to learn the intricacies and difficulties incident to success in this hazardous profession. It so proved. He lost his comfortable home on Fourth Street and also all of his little fortune in about three years, and died in 1854 a poor man.—(*Cincinnati Commercial.*)

※ ※ ※

Mrs. E. W. Guilford, widow of the late Nathan Guilford, philanthropist and founder of the common schools of Ohio, celebrated her eighty-first birthday yesterday. The reception was a remarkable one in many particulars, not only from the number of old citizens who paid their respects to the worthy hostess, but from the fact that the lady herself is such a well-preserved reminder of the old days in Cincinnati as to become an interesting link binding the present with the past. * * * Mrs. Guilford has been for sixty-seven years a resident of this city, and retains a fresh and delightful memory of the many changes that have taken place during that long period. She is an excellent conversationalist, and her recollections abound in a freshness and vividness that render them most interesting, while the easy grace and courtly polish of the old school are pleasantly discernible. There were about two hundred callers yesterday, numbering among them most of the old citizens of Cincinnati; * * * and each guest retired with heartfelt wishes that this honored lady may long enjoy the health and happiness to which a good and useful life has so much entitled her.—(*Cincinnati Paper*, August 13th, 1882.)

Mrs. Nathan Guilford, well known to a large circle of our older citizens, is now in her eighty-seventh year, but still retains the charm of manner and graceful bearing that made her one of the famous belles of this vicinity when Cincinnati was only an incipient city.—(*Cincinnati Commercial Gazette*, October 22d, 1887.)

The widow of Nathan Guilford is at the Grand Hotel, and is as remarkable for her grace and beauty now as she was half a century ago.—(*Cincinnati Enquirer*.)

Obituary.

Mrs. Eliza Wheeler Guilford died last night at the residence of her niece, Mrs. J. Paul, 273 West Fourth Street. Mrs. Guilford was the second daughter of Oliver Farnsworth, and was born in Newport, R. I., in 1801. When in her seventh year she removed with her parents to the town of Windsor, on the banks of the Connecticut River, where she lived until nearly seventeen, when her parents decided to leave the Green Mountain State and emigrate to the West. The destination they had in view was St. Louis, Mo. A spring wagon, a decided luxury in that day, comfortably bore the female portion of the family. After ninety-two consecutive days of travel the party reached Pittsburgh, where they embarked upon a vessel known in that day as a family boat. Twenty-one days more were consumed on the journey from Pittsburgh to Cincinnati, at the end of which time the boat was landed and tied up at what is now the foot of Main Street.

Cincinnati was a place of strangers to the wandering family, but they were given a most cordial reception, and the rare tidings were quickly proclaimed abroad of the arrival of a "family boat" with a Yankee family on board, in which were young ladies. The news created a sensation, and on the representation of influential citizens the travelers were induced to abandon their design of going to St. Louis and to remain in this city.

Mr. Farnsworth opened a publishing house and conducted it successfully for many years. In 1819 he published the first Cincinnati Directory, the city at that time having about seven thousand inhabitants.

Eliza Farnsworth was married to Nathan Guilford just one year from the day the family boat landed at this place. Like most educated Yankees, Mr. Guilford was an earnest advocate of the spreading of intelligence; in fact, he was best known through his hobby, as it was called, which was manifested in his unbounded enthusiasm for the education of the masses. To accomplish this object he spared neither pains, labor nor money. He was indefatigable in this pursuit, and left no means unemployed to gain the great end which he felt convinced would confer the greatest good upon the entire people—the establishment of free schools, supported by taxation on all real estate. Some of our people, we are told by old records, threatened to fight against so oppressive a measure, even to the point of the bayonet, but Mr. Guilford kept up his agitation for fourteen years, and finally carried his point against fierce opposition.

During these years of philanthropic struggling on the part of Mr. Guilford and his meagre array of friends to accomplish a beneficent end, he and they received the inspiring assistance and heroic support of his accomplished wife; and although the record has never been given much publicity, it is well known that much of the good gained, under adverse circumstances, was directly due to the strong but gentle influence of this estimable lady. During the latter years of her life she was fond of relating scenes and incidents of that period, and certainly no one could present them in a more entertaining or intelligent manner. Her memory was remarkably good, and her delightful manners, which retained much of their bright vivaciousness to the last—a beautiful reflection of the courtesy and solid polish of the old school—always rendered her reminiscences doubly charming.

NATHAN GUILFORD (2d)

From a photograph taken in 1876.

Mrs. Guilford has always resided in Cincinnati, with the exception of an occasional visit of a few weeks' duration to Washington or New York. The old Guilford homestead will be remembered as being situated on Fourth Street, west of Vine. It was a brick building of comfortable exterior and pleasant surroundings, and remained for many years a conspicuous object on the Fourth Street of the past. Mrs. Guilford was the mother of five children, two sons and three daughters, of whom the sons alone are living—William, who has for the past twenty years been engaged in the Treasury Department at Washington, and Nathan, the youngest of the family, who is General Traffic Manager of the New York Central Railroad at New York City.--(*Cincinnati Commercial Gazette*, February 24th, 1888.)

& *&* *&*

I, **NATHAN GUILFORD**, the present writer, was born in Cincinnati, February 7th, 1841. I went to school but little, but I profited more or less by home instruction and a natural taste for reading. At the age of twelve years I was sent to the preparatory department of Antioch College at Yellow Springs, Ohio—an excellent school for both sexes—of which the celebrated Horace Mann was President. There I got about all the "schooling" I ever had. In the midst of my second school-year I was called home by the death of my father.

Several years previously, attracted by the discovery of gold in California, my cousin, Henry Storrs Stone, had gone there to seek his fortune and had met with fair success. He had established a "general store" at Sonora, in the mining district of Tuolumne County, where he was doing a thriving trade. He invited me to join him there, and in the spring of 1856 I sailed from New York on the steamship "George Law" for Aspinwall, crossed the isthmus to Panama and there took the steamer "Golden Gate" for San Francisco, whence, by steamboat and stage,

I reached my destination after a journey of about four weeks. I remained there about eighteen months, when I determined to return to home and civilization. Shortly after my return I entered the office of Taft & Perry, at Cincinnati, as a law student, but a few months later, being offered employment in the freight office of the Little Miami Railroad, I abandoned the law, and since then (1859) have remained almost continuously in railroad service.

During the past twenty-five years I have held various official positions, among which are those of General Freight Agent of the Baltimore and Ohio Railroad, Commissioner of Railroad Associations, Vice-President of the New York and Manhattan Elevated Railroads, and General Traffic Manager of the New York Central & Hudson River Railroad. I have resided successively in Cincinnati, Columbus, O., Baltimore and New York City; and in April, 1883, I became a citizen of Yonkers, N. Y., which I have come to look upon as my permanent home.

Our great civil war broke out in April, 1861, and President Lincoln called for 75,000 volunteers to enlist for a term of three months, which period it was then thought would suffice to suppress the rebellion. Within an hour of the publication of the call I had enlisted, and the next morning was on my way to Washington as a private in the Second Ohio Volunteer Infantry. We were sent into Virginia, but when our term of enlistment had expired we had seen no fighting except some small skirmishing. We were at the front, and it was evident that an important battle was impending, so we volunteered to stay and "see it through." Some ten days later we were engaged in the memorable and disastrous battle of Bull Run, and soon after were mustered out and sent home.

Dwel ing in Yonkers N Y 1897

NATHAN GUILFORD (2d)

From a photograph taken in 1897.

In 1864 I again enlisted in response to a call for volunteers for a term of one hundred days. This time my regiment, the 137th Ohio National Guard, did only garrison duty, mostly at Fort McHenry, Baltimore.

On March 16th, 1865, I married Mary Jane Wallace, of Pittsburgh, Pa. Our children are:

1. Susan, born in Cincinnati, January 7th, 1866; died March 10th, 1866.
2. Nathan, born in Cincinnati, January 5th, 1867; married Helen M. Crooke, June 2d, 1891, who died March 10th, 1893.
3. Mary, born in Columbus, O., April 21st, 1872.
4. Wallace, born in Baltimore, Md., September 18th, 1873; married Josephine Louise deLoiselle, October 8th, 1897.
5. Gertrude, born in New York City, January 3d, 1880.

My only grandchild is Margaret Guilford, daughter of my son Nathan and Helen M. Crooke, born March 9th, 1893.

THE NORTON FAMILY.

❧ ❧ ❧

William Norton was admitted as a "freeman" of Hingham, Mass., March 3d, 1635–6.* He received (1635) from "the inhabitants of Hingham" a grant of land.† He died in Hingham in June, 1639.‡ Administration on his estate was granted to Ann, his wife, and their only daughter Susanna.§

Between 1638 and 1641 Ann Norton, "widow of William Norton," brought action against Samuel Ward, of Hingham, concerning a piece of meadow land.||

In June, 1649, Ann Norton, widow, married John Tucker, who died August 5th, 1661.¶

Widow Ann Tucker died October 8th, 1675. By her will she bequeaths the land in Hingham to her grandchildren, Paul and Susanna Guilford, children of her daughter, Susanna Norton, wife of John Guilford.*† Afterwards, in conveying part of this land to John Chubbuck, Paul Guilford describes it as part of that given to his grandfather, William Norton, by the inhabitants of Hingham.‡‡

---

* Col. Records i, 153; Hist. and Gen. Reg. ii, 194.
† Mentioned in Liber xiii, p. 258, Suffolk Co. Deeds.
‡ Hobart's Diary.
§ Suffolk Co. Probate, October 23d, 1667).
| Lincoln's History of Hingham, ii, 93.
¶ Savage's Gen. Dict.
*† Hist. of Hingham, iii, 269.
‡‡ Suff. Co. Deeds, xiii, 258.

There seem to have been two William Nortons—one who emigrated in the "Hopewell" in 1635, settled in Ipswich, married Lucy Downing, and died in 1694, aged 84 years; the other (our ancestor), a resident of Hingham in 1635, who died in 1639, his wife Ann surviving him. The first was brother of the Rev. John Norton, of Boston and Ipswich, a prominent Congregational minister, and "his genealogy is distinctly traced back to the time of William the Conqueror."* The two William Nortons may have been related, but I have found no evidence of it.

* N. E. Hist and Geneal. Reg., i, 78.

THE WHITNEY FAMILY.

✣ ✣ ✣

By far the greater number of Whitneys in the United States are descended from John Whitney who, in April, 1635 (aged 35), with his wife Elinor (30), embarked at Ipswich, England, on the "Elizabeth and Ann," Roger Cooper master, with five sons, viz.: John (aged 11,) Richard (9), Nathaniel (8), Thomas (6), and Jonathan (1), and in June, 1635, settled in Watertown, Mass. He was freeman March 3, 1636, selectman several times between 1638 and 1655, and town clerk 1655. He owned much property in Watertown. His wife, Elinor, died May 11th, 1659, and on September 29th of the same year he married Judith Clement. He died, a widower, June 1st, 1673.*

JOHN WHITNEY lived for a while at Isleworth, nine miles from London, where the parish records show the birth of three of his children. Among his descendants who have risen to distinction are Eli Whitney, the world-renowned inventor of the cotton gin; Professor William Dwight Whitney of Yale College, and Josiah Dwight Whitney, a geologist of the first rank.†

John Whitney, the emigrant, was son of Thomas Whitney, gentleman, of West Minster, and Mary Bray, his wife. He was descended from "Turstin the Fleming," or Sir Turstin de Wigmore, one of William the Conqueror's knights, who married Agnes, daughter of Alured de Merleberge, one of the great barons of the realm, who settled on her the Pencombe estate; and their descendant built a castle at Whitney, on the banks of the River Wye, in the twelfth century—whence the name.‡

* Bond's History of Watertown, p. 642.
† Whitney Genealogy, Introduction.
‡ Pierce's Genealogy of the Whitney Family, 1895.

THOMAS WHITNEY, fourth son of John and Elinor, was born in England in 1629, and on January 11th, 1654, married Mary Kedall. He lived at Watertown and Stow.

ELEAZER WHITNEY, son of Thomas, was born at Watertown April 7th, 1662. He was a wheelwright. He married April 11th, 1687, Dorothy Ross, daughter of James Ross, of Sudbury. She died June 22d, 1731.

THOMAS WHITNEY, son of Eleazer, was baptized at Sudbury, January 28th, 1699; married July 1st, 1720, Hannah Smith (born 1698). He was a farmer and lived at Shrewsbury and Marlboro. He died in 1748.

SUSANNA WHITNEY, daughter of Thomas, was baptized May 17th, 1729.*

Susanna Whitney married John Guilford, of Leicester, June 26th, 1750.

Mr. Ward, recording this marriage in his "History of Shrewsbury, Mass.", conjectures that the bride was "perhaps sister of Samuel Whitney," of Shrewsbury. The recently published genealogies of the Whitney family show the incorrectness of that assumption.

According to those elaborate genealogies there were living in 1750 but four Susanna Whitneys, and one "Anna" Whitney, whose baptismal name may have been Susanna—

> One, a sister of Samuel Whitney, of Shrewsbury. She was born 1707 and married Abraham Gregory in 1736.
>
> One, a daughter of Samuel, of Shrewsbury. She was born 1748 and married John Bellows in 1768.
>
> One, a daughter of John Whitney, of Westford. She was born 1730 and married John Dean.
>
> One (Anna), daughter of Nathaniel Whitney, of Weston. She was born 1730 and married David Forbush.

* Pierce's Genealogy.

One, daughter of Thomas, of Shrewsbury and Marlboro, born 1729. Her husband's name is not shown in any of the genealogies; but since John Guilford married in 1750 Susanna Whitney, of Shrewsbury, his wife could have been no other than Thomas's daughter—all the other Susannas then living having been provided with other husbands.

Susanna Whitney was a most superior woman, of great energy, and an ardent patriot. Her three eldest sons were revolutionary soldiers. It is related of her that when her son Asa was ill of typhoid fever, in camp at Cambridge, she rode horseback sixty miles to nurse him; and when he died, and his body, wrapped in the blanket on which she had ridden, had been interred in a soldier's grave, she returned as she had come.

THE HOBBS FAMILY.

❧ ❧ ❧

JOSIAH HOBBS was born in England in 1649, and emigrated on the "Arabella" from Gravesend May 27th, 1671, settled in Boston, and moved to Lexington in 1690. He married in 1683 Tabitha —— He was a soldier in King Philip's War, serving in Captain Joseph Sill's Company (June, 1676). He had seven children, of whom only his son Josiah lived to marry. He died in Lexington, Mass., May 30th, 1741, aged 92 years. He was of slight figure, and below the medium size.

JOSIAH HOBBS, his son, was born in Boston in 1684, moved to Lexington in 1690, returned to Boston in 1705, and settled in Weston in 1730. He was a strict and austere Puritan, and joined Cotton Mather's church. He married Esther Davenport (born Feb. 11th, 1691, died Nov. 29th, 1778), daughter of Ebenezer Davenport, of Dorchester, and his wife, Dorcas Andrews, daughter of James Andrews, of Falmouth. Josiah died Feb. 27th, 1779, aged 95 years.

JOHN HOBBS, son of Josiah, was born at Governor's Island in Boston Harbor in 1721. He lived at Weston in 1743 and moved thence to Brookfield. He was a revolutionary soldier in Captain Asa Danforth's Company, Colonel Conver's regiment in General Gates' Army in 1777; was present at Burgoyne's defeat; was taken ill from exposure in the field and returned to Brookfield, where he died in 1777. He married in 1744 Beulah Warren, by whom he had eight children :

1. Beulah, born 1747, died 1817; married Isaac Warren, of Sturbridge. Children: (1) Roswell, (2) John, (3) Isaac, (4) George, (5) Sally.
2. Lydia, ⎫ Twins, born 1760. Betsy died unmarried in Brook-
3. Betsy, ⎭ field in 1850, aged 90 years.
4. Jesse, born 1762, died 1840. Resided in Brookfield.
5. Allan, —— —— Settled in Spencer.
6. Daniel, born about 1767, died 1847.
7. Ruth, —— died unmarried.
8. Anna, —— died unmarried.

LYDIA HOBBS, daughter of John, was born in 1760, and died in 1848, aged 88. She married in 1783 Dr. Jonas Guilford, of Spencer.

THE WARREN FAMILY.

❧ ❧ ❧

JOHN WARREN, was born in England in 1585. He emigrated to America with his wife Margaret —— and several children in 1630 and settled in Watertown, Mass. Was freeman May 18th, 1631; selectman, 1636 to 1640. In 1635 he and Abraham Browne were appointed to lay out all highways and see that they were repaired. In 1642 he owned eight lots containing 176 acres. In 1651 he was fined twenty shillings for an offence against the laws of baptism. On April 4th, 1654, he was fined for neglect of public worship, 14 sabbaths at five shillings each, £3.10. In 1658-9 he was ordered to be warned for not attending public worship. May 27th, 1661, he was charged with harboring Quakers, and his house was ordered to be searched. His wife, Margaret, died November 6th, 1662; he died December 13th, 1667, aged 82 years. His will mentions the following children, probably all born in England: John, born 1622; Mary, who in 1642 married John Bigelow; Daniel, born 1628, and Elizabeth, who, about 1654, married James Knapp.*

DANIEL WARREN, son of John, born in England 1628, married in 1650 Mary Barron (died 1715), daughter of Ellis Barron, who was freeman of Watertown, June 2d, 1641; constable 1658; selectman 1668 and 1673. Ellis Barron died October 30th, 1676. His wife was named Grace ——. Daniel Warren was a soldier in King Philip's War in Captain Nathaniel Davenport's Company, November, 1675;† in Capt. Joseph Sill's Company, December, 1675, and in Capt. John Cutler's Co., July 1776.‡

* Bond's Watertown, p. 620.
† Mass. Archives, 68–100.
‡ Bodge, 272–286.

The following document is published in *Bodge's Soldiers of King Philip's War, p.* 227:

"Petition of Daniel Warren and Joseph Peirce To inform the Honoured Counsel of the service don at Sudbury by severall of the Inhabatance of Watertown as our honoured Captain Mason hath Allready informed a part thereof in the petion: but we who wear thear can moer largely inform this honoured counsel: that as it said in the petion that we drove two hundred Indians over the River: we followed the enemie over the river and joyned with som others and went to see if wee could relieve Captain Wadsworth upon the hill and thear we had a fight with the Indians but they being soe many of them and we stayed soe long that we wear almost incompassed by them which cased us to retreat to Captain Goodanons Garrison: and their we stayed it being ner night till it was dark and then we went to Mr. Noices Mill to see if we could find any that were escaped to that place all though they wear noe persons dwelling thear: but thear we found: 13: or: 14: of Captain Wadsworths men who wear escaped some of them wounded and brought them to Sudbury towne: On the next day in the morning soe soon as it was light we went to looke for Concord men who wear slain in the river middow and thear we went in the colld water up to the Knees where we found five and we brought them in comes to the Bridge fut and buried them thear: and then we joyned ourselves to Captain Hunton with as many others as we could procuer and went over the river to look for Captain Wadsworth and Captain Brattlebank and the soldiers that wear slain: and we gathered them up and Buried them: and then it was agreed that we should goe up to Nobscot to bring the Carts from thence into Sudbury Towne and soe returned Hom againe: to what is above written we whos nams are subscribed can testifi   dated the: 6: of march   78 Daniel Warrin
79 Josep Peirce

Our request is to the much Honoured Counsel that they would be pleased to consider us in reference to our Request: their being 2 troops of hors appointed to bury the dead as we wear informed whos charg was spared and we as yet not allowed for what we did.

Your most Humble Servants to Command to the utmost of our poor S for our selves and in behalf of the rest.*

* Mass. Archives, Vol. lxviii, p. 224.

Ensign **JOHN WARREN**, son of Daniel Warren, was born 1665 and died 1703. He married (1682) Mary Browne. They had two children:
1. John (known as Deacon John Warren).
2. Jonathan.

Mary Warren, daughter of Daniel and sister of Ensign John, married Nathaniel Fiske.

Deacon **JOHN WARREN**, of Weston, Mass., was born March 15th, 1684-5, and died March 25th, 1745. He married (June 2d, 1708) Abigail Livermore.

BEULAH WARREN, of Weston, daughter of Deacon John and Abigail (Livermore) Warren, was born Aug. 23d, 1725, and in 1744 married John Hobbs.

THE LIVERMORE FAMILY.

❧ ❧ ❧

PETER LIVERMORE was born at Little Thurloe, County Suffolk, England, and was buried there November 16th, 1611. He married (June 5th, 1594) Marabella Wysbyck, who was buried at Little Thurloe July 12th, 1612.

JOHN LIVERMORE, their son, was baptized at Little Thurloe September 30th, 1604. He embarked in April, 1634, from Ipswich in the "Francis," John Cutting master. His wife, Grace, was the daughter of Edmond Sherman, of Dedham, County Suffolk, England, who was born in 1595 and came to New England in 1634. She followed her husband to America with their daughter Hannah (born 1633). John Livermore moved to Watertown, Mass., in 1639, thence to Wethersfield, Conn., where he owned land in 1640; thence back to Watertown. He was freeman in 1635, and was frequently selectman. He died at Watertown April 4th, 1682, aged 78. His wife, Grace, died in 1690. They had nine children.

SAMUEL LIVERMORE, their son, married (June 4th, 1668) Anna Bridge (born 1646, died 1727), daughter of Matthew Bridge, of Cambridge (died 1700) and his wife Anna Danforth, and granddaughter of Deacon John Bridge, who is recorded as living in Cambridge in 1632, and who died in 1665. Samuel Livermore had twelve children, of whom his daughter, Abigail (born October 9th, 1683, died October 31st, 1743) married (June 2d, 1708) Deacon John Warren, of Weston.

THE DANFORTH FAMILY.

NICHOLAS DANFORTH emigrated in 1634 from Framlingham, County Suffolk, England, where he had a manor and considerable property, and settled in Watertown, Mass., where he died in April, 1638. He was freeman March 3d, 1636, and representative 1636–7. "He was a distinguished protector of Puritanism in New England."[*]

The Framlingham lectures were founded by him. His wife Elizabeth died in England in 1629.

ANNA DANFORTH, his second child, was born in England about 1620 and died December 2d, 1704. She married (1643-4) Matthew Bridge, of Cambridge. They had seven children, of whom their daughter Anna (born 1646) married Samuel Livermore.

[*] N. E. H. & G. Reg., vi, 279.

THE FARNSWORTH FAMILY.

✗ ✗ ✗

This name was formerly spelled "Farnworth" (pronounced Farnoth). The family came from England, probably from Lancashire. The s was introduced about 1750. The name was probably derived from "fearn" (A.-S.) fern, and "worth," a landed estate.

MATTHIAS FARNSWORTH is recorded as a resident of Lynn, Mass., in 1657. When he came to this country is not known. Several years later he moved to Groton, Mass., where his name appears as an original proprietor. He married Mary Farr, daughter of George Farr, a shipwright of Lynn, who emigrated from London in 1629. He filled various offices in the town and was a prominent church member. He died in January, 1689, leaving a will in which he calls himself "aged about 77 yers," which would make the year of his birth 1611. Matthias had eleven children, as follows:

1. Elizabeth, born 1647, died 1729; married January 16th, 1667, James Robinson. Had one child, Elizabeth, born October 3d, 1668, married January 4th, 1685, William Lakin, of Groton.

2. Matthias, born about 1649, died about 1693; married about 1681, Sarah, daughter of John Nutting. Was a soldier in King Philip's War under Major Willard. His children were Joseph, Ebenezer, Josiah and Matthias.

3. John, born about 1651, died 1729; married 1686, Hannah Aldis, of Dedham; had nine children—Abigail, John, Daniel, Nathan, Joseph, Jeremiah, Hannah, Rachel and Sarah.

4. Benjamin, born about 1653, married 1695, Mary, daughter of Jonas Prescott. Their children were Mary, Martha, Benjamin, Isaac, Ezra, Amos, Lydia, Aaron, Martha and Jonas.

5. Joseph, born 1657, died 1674.

6. Mary, born 1660, died 1725; married 1676, Samuel Thatcher, of Watertown. Their ten children were Mary, Samuel, John, Anna, Mary, Hannah, Abigail, Mercy, Sarah and Ebenezer.

7. Sarah, born 1664, died 1731; married Simon Stone, of Watertown. Their children were Sarah, Simon, Abigail, Susanna, Isaac, Hannah, Lydia, Joseph and Benjamin.

8. Samuel.

9. Abigail, born 1671, married John Hutchins. Their children were John, Joshua, Abigail, Elizabeth and Benjamin.

10. Jonathan, born 1675, died 1748; married 1698, Ruth Shattuck. Their fifteen children were Ruth, Jonathan, Ephraim, Reuben, Phineas, Priscilla, Nathaniel, John, Hannah, Simeon, Susanna, Elias, John, Silas and Betty.

11. Joseph, born ——— died 1687.

SAMUEL FARNSWORTH, eighth child of Matthias, was born at Groton, Oct. 8th, 1669. He married, December 12th, 1706, Mary Whitcomb Willard, daughter of Josiah Whitcomb, of Lancaster (who was a Deputy to the General Court in 1710, and who commanded the garrison at Lancaster in 1711), and widow of Simon Willard, Jr. Samuel subsequently moved to the "Turkey Hills" (now Lunenburg). He was a member of the Groton church. He died in 1727. He had six children:

1. Mary Crew, born 1707, married 1727, Jonathan Page of Turkey Hills (Lunenburg).

2. Samuel, born 1709, died 1746, unmarried.

3. David, born 1711, married 1735, Hannah Hastings, of Lunenburg. They had six children, two sons and four daughters. Their fifth child, Samuel (born 1750), was a drummer at the battle of Bunker Hill, and was ancestor of two distinguished Brigadier-Generals of cavalry in the civil war, Generals John F. and Elon J. Farnsworth.

4. Abigail, born 1713.

5. Stephen.

6. Joshua, born 1721, died unmarried.

STEPHEN FARNSWORTH, fifth child of Samuel, was born at Lunenburg in 1715. He married Eunice Hastings, of Watertown, Mass., December 22d, 1741. She was a sister of his brother David's wife, and was descended from Thomas Hastings, who emigrated from England in 1634. Stephen was one of the first settlers of Charlestown, N. H., and one of the original members of the church there. He was taken prisoner by the Indians in 1746 and escaped, but was again taken prisoner by them August 29th, 1754, when a party of fifty St. Francis Indians came across from Crown Point, on Lake Champlain, surprised the settlers, plundered and burned the village, and carried Farnsworth and three other captives to Canada. He was not released for seventeen months. He died September 6th, 1771. About two years later his widow sold her property in Charlestown, and with several of her children settled in South Woodstock, Vt., where she died June 7th, 1811, aged 88 years. Their four children were:

1. Oliver.

2. Jonathan, married twice. His children were: Polly, Patty, Brewer and Sally; and by his second wife, Susan ———, were: Azuba, Oliver, Susan and Ann.

3. Stephen, had twelve children: Fanny, Enos, Terah, Ora, Lotty, Laura, Elon, Aurelia, Stephen, Deborah, John and Harriet.

4. Polly, married —— Standish. Had no children.

OLIVER FARNSWORTH, eldest son of Stephen, was born at Charlestown, N. H., December 18th, 1742, and is recorded as " the first child born in the old fort." On July 6th, 1768, he married Elizabeth Wheeler, daughter of Moses and Elizabeth Wheeler of that town. He afterwards removed to Woodstock, Vt., where in 1773 he bought 420 acres of land, and from that time onward he was elected to various offices—town clerk, selectman, etc. His house occupying a central and convenient position, town meetings were generally held there. On May 7th, 1777, he enlisted as private soldier in Col. Benj. Bellows' regiment in the Northern Continental Army, and was discharged June 18th. He again enlisted July 21st, 1777, in Captain Abel Walker's Company of Col. David Hobart's regiment in Gen. Stark's brigade, and was discharged September 23d, 1777.* He was killed by a falling tree in 1786; and the "History of Woodstock " says "his death was felt to be a great loss to the infant settlement" His widow married a Rev. Mr. Norton, whom she survived. She died in her 98th year. Oliver had six children, as follows:

1. Abiel, who had one son, Alden Farnsworth, who settled in St. Charles, Mo.

2. Havilah, born 1769, who was a practising physician in Newport, R. I., and had four children: Havilah, Caroline, Minerva and Francis, who in 1818 were living in Euclid, O.

3. Abijah, who had six children : Oliver, Elijah, Esther, Betsey Abijah and Samson.

* New Hampshire Revolutionary Rolls. Vol. II, pp. 11-141.

4. Betsey, who married —— Lathrop, a Baptist minister. Betsey, the eldest of their six children, removed to Troy, N. Y., about 1817.

5. Phoebe, who married —— Reed ; had no children.

6. Oliver.

OLIVER FARNSWORTH (2d) was born at Woodstock December 10th, 1775. He became a printer, and in 1797 began publishing a newspaper at Suffield, Conn., called "The Impartial Herald." In 1798 he, with his brother Havilah, opened a printing office in Newport, R. I., where in 1799 Oliver began to publish the "Rhode Island Republican," a Jeffersonian newspaper, which brought upon him the most violent abuse of William Cobbett in the "Porcupine Papers." In 1800 he published a life of Washington, the first attempt in that direction after Washington's death. The title reads: "A Memory of Washington ; Comprising a Sketch of His Life and Character and the National Testimonials of Respect. Also a Collection of Eulogies and Orations, with a Copious Appendix. Newport, R. I. Printed by Oliver Farnsworth, 1800."

Oliver married Anne, daughter of Paul Mumford, by whom he had seven children, born between 1799 and 1811. About 1808 they removed to Windsor, Vt., where, in 1809, with General Sylvester Churchill, he established the "Vermont Republican."

In 1818, Oliver, with his family, emigrated to what was then the "far west." On his way down the Ohio River their house-boat halted at Cincinnati, where they were greeted by NATHAN GUILFORD, a young lawyer, recently become a resident of that place. He was so deeply impressed with the attractions of their daughter,

OLIVER FARNSWORTH (2d).

From a miniature in the possession of Mrs. J. Paul.

ELIZA FARNSWORTH GUILFORD.

From a portrait painted about 1819.

ELIZA WHEELER FARNSWORTH, that he strongly urged them to abandon their purpose of going farther, and to make Cincinnati their home. This they were persuaded to do, and Oliver opened the first printing office and published the first newspaper in that region. His wife, Anne, died in 1850, in her eightieth year; and in his old age Oliver returned to Newport, where he died September 23d, 1859, in his eighty-fourth year. Their children were:

1. Anne Maria, born December 7th, 1799, who married Louis F. Gallup, of Woodstock. Her second husband was Phineas Page.

2. Eliza Wheeler, born August 12th, 1801; married October 28th, 1819, Nathan Guilford, of Cincinnati.

3. William Mumford, born April 28th, 1803, died in 1885; married Lavinia Brittain, of Urbana, Ohio; moved to Springfield, Ill., where he was State Printer for many years.

4. Oliver, born March 13th, 1805, died in 1841.

5. Jane H., born May 28th, 1806, died in 1816.

6. Augusta Mumford, born March 8th, 1808; married in 1824, Dan Stone, of Cincinnati, who became an intimate friend of Abraham Lincoln, and his partner in the practise of law. Their children were:

    1. Jane, born September 7th, 1826, and now (1897) living in Toledo, O. She married (1) Calmes Wight, an officer in the Mexican war and (2) Josiah Paul. Her two sons are Calmes T. Wight who married Henrietta Speyer, and Charles S. Wight who married (1) Ella Guild and (2) Anna Mauthe. 2. Charles, born July 1828, died February, 1842. 3. Henry Storrs, born June, 1830; married in 1886, Mary Hannum; now living in San Francisco. 4. Apolline, born December 23d, 1836; married Fayette Smith, of Cincinnati; died April 1st, 1874. Her surviving children are (1) Constance, married Joseph Homer, of Boston; (2) Royal S., married Lillian Blauvelt; (3) Goldsborough.

7. Paul Mumford, born September 28th, 1811, died about 1873; married Martha Fulton, of Cincinnati. His two children, William and Charles, removed to California.

The foregoing notes on the Farnsworth family are derived partly from family records and town histories, but mostly from a book entitled "*Matthias Farnsworth and his Descendants*," published in 1891 by Claudius Buchanan Farnsworth, of Pawtucket, who boasts that in his search of half a century for genealogical material for his book, "the prison and the almshouse have contributed no names to the record."

THE HASTINGS FAMILY.

THOMAS HASTINGS, born in England in 1605, and his first wife, Susanna, sailed from Ipswich April 10th, 1634, in the ship "Elizabeth," Wm. Andrews, master, and settled in Watertown, Mass. He was freeman 1635, selectman many times, town clerk 1670-71 and was long a deacon. His wife died February 2d, 1650, and in 1651 he married Margaret Cheney. He died in 1685. Their second son,

JOHN HASTINGS, was born in Watertown March 1st, 1653, and died March 28th, 1718. On June 18th, 1679, he married Abigail Hammond, of Watertown (born June 21st, 1659, died April 7th, 1718). She was a daughter of Lieut. John Hammond, and great-granddaughter of Thomas Hammond, of Cavenham, County Suffolk, England. Their eldest son and second child,

JOHN HASTINGS, was born about 1683 and died previous to 1747. He married January 8th, 1706, Sarah Fiske (born July 4th, 1684), daughter of Nathaniel Fiske, of Watertown, and of the sixth generation in descent from Robert Fiske, of Broad Gates, near Framlingham, County Suffolk, England. Their daughter,

EUNICE HASTINGS (born Sept. 3d, 1722, died June 9th, 1811), married (December 22d, 1741) Stephen Farnsworth. It is recorded that "on the day of her marriage she was admitted to full communion of the church in Lunenburg."

THE HAMMOND FAMILY.

THOMAS HAMMOND, of Cavenham, County Suffolk, England, married (May 14th, 1573) Rose Trippe. He died in November, 1589. Their son,

WILLIAM HAMMOND, of Cavenham, was baptized October 30th, 1575. He emigrated to New England previous to 1634 and settled in Watertown, Mass. He married, in England (June 9th, 1605), Elizabeth Payne, who followed him in April, 1634, in the ship "Francis," from Ipswich, with their children—she aged 47; their daughter Elizabeth, 15; Sarah, 10, and John, aged 7 years. William was freeman in 1636 and selectman in 1648. He died in 1662, and his widow, Elizabeth, died in 1670.

JOHN HAMMOND, their son, known as Lieut. John Hammond, was born in 1627. His first wife, Sarah, the mother of his children, was born in 1643 and died January 14th, 1688. He died Nov. 22d, 1709. In 1690 his assessment for taxes was the largest in the town.

ABIGAIL HAMMOND, the fourth child of Lieut. John Hammond, was born June 21st, 1659, and died April 7th, 1718. On June 18th, 1679, she was married to John Hastings, Sr.

THE FISKE FAMILY.

ROBERT FISKE, of Broad Gates, near Framlingham, County Suffolk, England, married Sibil Gould. They had three sons, William, Jeffrey and Thomas. The record of the sons' children is wanting, but we find that William had two grandsons, John and William Fiske; that Jeffrey had a grandson, David Fiske, and that Thomas had two grandsons, James and Phineas Fiske.

NATHAN FISKE, son of one of the aforesaid grandsons, and great-grandson of Robert Fiske, settled in Watertown in 1642; was freeman in 1643 and selectman in 1673. He died June 21st, 1676. His wife was named Susanna.

NATHANIEL FISKE, fourth son of Nathan (born July 12th, 1653, died 1735), married (April 13th, 1677) Mary Warren, widow of John Child, and daughter of Daniel and Mary (Barron) Warren.

SARAH FISKE, daughter of Nathaniel and Mary, was born July 4th, 1684, and married (January 8th, 1706) John Hastings, Jr. Their daughter, Eunice, married Stephen Farnsworth.

THE MUMFORD FAMILY.

❧ ❧ ❧

THOMAS MUMFORD emigrated from England, presumably from London, as he was in all probability nearly related to one Stephen Mumford, who is known to have come from London, and some of whose descendants and those of Thomas intermarried. He settled in Portsmouth and moved to South Kingstown, R. I., near Newport, where he appears to have been a man of substance, and is recorded as holding various offices. December 10th, 1657, he had a grant of eight acres. January 20th, 1658, he and others bought a large tract in Pettaquamscutt of certain Indian sachems.

May 5th, 1664, he was ordered released from prison on giving bonds of £100 "to appear when called to speak further to matter concerning Timothy Mather, whom he had accused for speaking words of a very dishonourable nature against His Majesty."

June 20th, 1670, he was constable, and was ordered by the Assembly "to seize any persons found exercising jurisdiction in Narragansett in behalf of the Colony of Connecticut." He must have acted promptly under this order, for June 21st he was complained of by the Commissioners of Connecticut for assaulting and detaining "two of our men who were inoffensively riding on the King's highway."

He was again constable 1683–86 and grand juror 1687–88. October 30th, 1690, he was appointed by the

Assembly, with three others, to fix the tax rate for King's Town. He married Sarah Odding Sherman, of Roxbury, Mass. (born 1636, died 1719). Their children were :

1. Thomas.
2. Peleg.
3. Abigail.
4. Sarah.

He died intestate before February 12th, 1692.

THOMAS MUMFORD (2d), (born 1656, died 1726), was a large landholder and prominent citizen; was a deputy in 1701 and justice of the peace in 1707. The records of the Colony show that he deeded many hundreds of acres of land in his lifetime. His wife Abigail —————— (1670–1707) was murdered by one of her negro slaves. The journal of the Assembly shows the following action of that body at its session on May 28th, 1707 :

> WHEREAS, the wife of Thomas Mumford having been murdered about two weeks since by a slave belonging to him, and the body of the negro having since been found upon the shore of Little Compton (he having drowned himself as was believed to prevent being taken alive), it is ordered by the Assembly that his head, legs and arms be cut from his body and hung up in some public place near Newport, and his body to be burned to ashes, that it may be something of a terror to others from perpetrating of the like barbarity for the future.

In November, 1708, Thomas married Esther Tefft. He died in April, 1726; he and his first wife were buried in the Mumford burial ground. Their children were ·

1. Thomas, born 1687.
2. George, born 1689.
3. Joseph, born 1691.
4. William, born 1694.
5. Benjamin, born 1696.
6. Richard, born 1698.

WILLIAM MUMFORD, of South Kingstown, R. I. (born February 18th, 1694), married April 3d, 1729, Ann Wilson (widow Ray), who was born at Block Island December 7th, 1702, and was the daughter of Jeremiah Wilson (1674–1740)—(of whom Thomas Mumford was guardian)—and granddaughter of Samuel Wilson (1622–1682), of Portsmouth and Kingstown, R. I.   There was another William Mumford living at Newport, probably a descendant of Stephen previously mentioned, who was made a freeman of Newport in 1721, while Thomas's son William was made a freeman of South Kingstown, R. I., in 1722.   South Kingstown being practically a suburb of Newport and the two Williams being contemporaries, the identity of names is confusing.

The historical records of Rhode Island show that a William Mumford was " Master of the Alienation Office " in 1730 ; that one of that name was Deputy for Newport in 1753, 1756 and 1757 ; that in 1758 " Captain William Mumford" was appointed by the General Assembly to superintend the construction of Fort George on Goat Island, Newport Harbor (the present torpedo station), and to disburse an appropriation of 10,000 pounds ster ling made for that purpose.   We cannot with certainty determine whether any or all of these offices were held by our ancestor or by the other William.

The children of William, of South Kingstown, and Ann, were :

1. Nathaniel, born 1729.
2. Abigail, born 1731.
3. Paul, born 1734.
4. Sarah, born 1737.
5. Simon Ray, born 1739.
6. Gideon, born 1741.
7. Augustus, born 1744.

GOV. PAUL MUMFORD.
From a portrait in the Redwood Library, Newport, R. I.

PAUL MUMFORD (born March 5th, 1734, died July 20th, 1805) married at Trinity Church, Newport, February 3d, 1769, Mary Maylem, who was a daughter of the Reverend John Maylem (1694-1742), of Harvard College (1715), and who was born in Boston August 12th, 1737. Paul is recorded as a member of the alumni of Yale College. He acted a prominent part in public affairs during and after the revolutionary period.

The "Records of the Colony of Rhode Island" show that in 1775 he was appointed by the General Assembly one of a committee of four "to examine the prisoners taken into custody by General Hopkins and make report to the Assembly as soon as may be." In 1777 he was returned as deputy from Newport and also from Barrington, "where he had purchased an estate and taken up his residence." The same year he was appointed to attend a convention at Springfield called "to consider the subject of the currency and the defence of Rhode Island," and the General Assembly ordered to be paid to him "for his time, his servant, two horses and carriage and expenses to Springfield, 18 pounds." In 1779 he was appointed by the General Assembly a member of the Council of War. In 1782 the same body ordered that "43 pounds, 4s. 8d. silver money be paid out of the General Treasury to Paul Mumford, Esquire, as the value of a negro slave belonging to him that enlisted in Col. Green's regiment in 1778." In 1779 and 1780 he was appointed assistant to the Governor. From 1778 to 1781 he was Associate Justice, and from 1781 to 1788 Chief Justice of the Supreme Court. In 1785 he was elected a delegate to Congress, and in 1803 Lieutenant-Governor; and the Governor, Arthur Fenner, dying in that year, was succeeded by Paul Mumford, who also died in office.

In private life Paul Mumford is said to have been a man of strong will and intense prejudices, proud of his name and political honors. An uncompromising aristocrat, he held the " common herd" in sovereign contempt. The children of Paul Mumford were :

1. William, born February 6th, 1770, who, according to family tradition, was a sea captain.
2. Anne Maylem, born June 30th, 1771.
3. Paul Maylem, a writer of political pamphlets, which indicate that he was a political "crank." He was a resident of Newport in 1819, and in 1827 was living in Smithfield, R. I., when he published one of his screeds which is preserved in the public library at Newport. In it he incidentally refers to his family, saying : " A truer friend than my father—more vigilant or devoted—the people of this State or of any State never knew." He mentions his mother as a native of Boston and her father as "a minister of the gospel," and says of her brother John Maylem, 2nd (born 1739), who wrote a poem on the siege of Louisbourg, that he was an adjutant in the Old French War and author of two much admired poems on that war. Family tradition says that Paul, Jr., died insane.

Governor Paul Mumford's marriage to Mary Maylem appears to have been his second marriage, as indicated by the following record · " Married in East Greenwich by John Olive, Justice, May 4th, 1762, Paul Mumford, son of William Mumford, of South Kingstown, to Mary Fry." This Mary Fry was born February 26th, 1742-3, and was daughter of John and Elizabeth Fry.

By his will, made three weeks before his death, Gov. Paul bequeaths to his wife " the furniture and notes she brought with her," in lieu of dower ; to his daughter Anne Maylem five hundred dollars in cash, certain

ANNE MUMFORD FARNSWORTH.

From a miniature in the possession of Mrs. J. Paul.

household furniture, her husband's note for $1,278, and one-third of a certain lot of land in Newport; to his son William, one-third of the same lot, another lot with buildings thereon and two thousand and fifty dollars in money; and to his son Paul Maylem the family residence in Newport, 130 acres of woodland in South Kingstown, and all the rest and residue of his estate.

The accompanying portrait of Gov. Paul Mumford is from a photograph of an oil painting now hanging in the Redwood Library, Newport, R. I., which received it from Avis C. Mumford, who was descended from both the emigrants, Thomas and Stephen Mumford.

ANNE MAYLEM MUMFORD was born in 1771, as above, and died in Springfield, Ill., in 1850. In 1798 she married Oliver Farnsworth.

Our genealogical tables show a long array of English names. The Farnsworths and Guilfords were fair and of the Saxon type; Anne Mumford, like her father, was of dark olive complexion, with bright black, almond-shaped eyes. She was warm of temper, sharp of tongue, strong of will and of bright intelligence. Some of her personal characteristics she transmitted in a marked degree to her descendants, and the Mumford eyes and complexion may be easily recognized in a number of her great-grandchildren, only a small proportion of whose blood is derived from her.

The Mumford coat-of-arms was "a lion, rampant, on a green field, thirteen crossed crosslets, and a turbot's head." It was engraved on a seal of Paul Mumford's worn by my cousin Henry Storrs Stone, who lost it while traveling in Europe.

THE SHERMAN FAMILY.

❧ ❧ ❧

THOMAS SHERMAN, of County Suffolk, England, was buried at Dedham, England, March 16th, 1564.

HENRY SHERMAN, his son (born 1520, died 1589), married Agnes Butler, who died 1580.

HENRY SHERMAN, his son, married Susan Hills; they both died in 1610.

SAMUEL SHERMAN, his son (born 1573, died 1615), married Phillis Ward, who survived him.

PHILIP SHERMAN, his son, born at Dedham, February 5th, 1610, emigrated in 1633 to Roxbury, Mass., where he is recorded as freeman same year. He married Sarah Odding, of Roxbury. Having become a partisan of Ann Hutchinson, he, with one hundred and seventeen others, was banished from Massachusetts Bay, October 2d, 1637. In 1638 he, with John Clark and others, bought "the island of Rhode Island" (Newport) from Aquetnet, an Indian chief. "They named the upper part of it Portsmouth, and there Sherman resided, owning a large tract of land. He held various public offices in the colony, and as a man of intelligence, wealth and influence was frequently consulted by those in authority"* Sherman became a Quaker; was the first secretary of Providence Plantations (1639), member Court of Commissioners (1656) and deputy (1665-7). He died in 1687.

The Sherman coat-of-arms was, on shield or, a lion rampant, sable, between three oak leaves, vert.

SARAH SHERMAN, daughter of Philip, was born in Roxbury in 1636, died 1719. She married Thomas Mumford.

NOTE.—Roger Sherman, signer of the Declaration of Independence, was descended from the same family of Dedham, England.—(*N. E. Hist. & Gen. Register.*)

* Talcott's Notes of New England Families.

THE WILSON FAMILY.

SAMUEL WILSON, of Portsmouth and Kingstown, R. I., was born 1622 and died 1682. He married Tabitha, daughter of John Tefft, who died in 1676, and Mary, his wife, who died in 1679. He was freeman in 1655.

JEREMIAH WILSON, of New Shoreham (now Block Island), Newport and South Kingstown, was third child of Samuel, and was born in 1674 and died June 2d, 1740. He married (1st), December 8th, 1700, Ann Manoxon, and (2d), Mary ———. Their daughter Ann was born in New Shoreham December 7th, 1702. In his will he bequeaths £50 to "daughter Ann Mumford, wife of William Mumford." Thomas Mumford, Senior, in 1694 was guardian of Samuel Wilson's children, and of Jeremiah especially.*

ANN WILSON, daughter of Jeremiah, born 1702, married (1st), ——— Ray. On April 3d, 1729, she married William Mumford at Trinity Church, Newport.

* Geneal. Dict. of Rhode Island, p. 136.

THE MAYLEM FAMILY.

The Reverend **JOHN MAYLEM**, was born about 1694; was graduated at Harvard College 1715; was freeman of Newport, R. I., 1740. He died in 1742. His children were:

1. Ann.
2. Mary.
3. Francis. } All of whom died in early childhood.
4. Brackett.
5. Keziah.
6. Rachel.
7. Mary.
8. John, who was an officer in the Old French War, and wrote two poems on the war.

MARY MAYLEM, seventh child of John, was born in Boston, August 12th, 1737, and on February 3d, 1769, married Paul Mumford.

JUDGE GEORGE WALLACE.

From a miniature on ivory.

THE WALLACE FAMILY

❧ ❧ ❧

GEORGE WALLACE, of Braddock's Field, Pa., was the first Judge of the Court of Common Pleas of Allegheny County, Pa., being commissioned by Benjamin Franklin. His portrait is preserved in the new courthouse at Pittsburgh. He was a man of prominence and considerable possessions. His estate of Braddock's Field was the scene of General Braddock's memorable defeat in 1755. He married Jane ———, and died in 1810, leaving nine children, all born on the Braddock estate, viz.:

1. Thomas.

2. George (2d), who married Jane Gibson, daughter of Chief Justice Gibson, of Indiana. George died in 1826, and his widow married Zara Costen. She died in 1864, leaving no children by either marriage.

3. Irvin, who married Julia Duncan, of Carlisle, Pa., and had six children.

4. Arabella, who married Daniel Beltzhoover. Of their four children, three—George, Melchore and Henry—died unmarried ; their daughter Eliza married ——— Swasey, of Natchez, Miss.

5. Charles, who married Maria Peters, of Pittsburgh.

6. Eliza, who married Judge Reeves, of Chillicothe, Ohio.

7. Harry, who removed to Kentucky.

8. Lewis.

9. William, who married Jane Elliott, of Wilkinsburg, Pa.

THOMAS WALLACE, eldest son of George, married Mary Boggs, of Pittsburgh, who died in 1832. Their four children were :

1. Jane, who married Adams McFadden. They had two daughters, Mary, who married Robert Brooke, of New York, and Jane (unmarried).

2. George (3d.)

3. James R., who died unmarried in 1835.

4. Martha, who died unmarried in 1833.

GEORGE WALLACE, eldest son of Thomas, was born at Pittsburgh in 1810, and on February 12th, 1835, married Susanna Cook, of Philadelphia. He died in 1851, leaving three daughters, viz.:

1. Martha, born at Pittsburgh, April 12th, 1836; died, unmarried, August 7th, 1859.

2. Mary Jane.

3. Arabella, born July 8th, 1844; married Mansfield Walworth Davison, of Saratoga, N. Y. Their children are :

    (1) Frances Wallace, born at Saratoga, N. Y., November 23d, 1870; (2) Sara Walworth, born at Saratoga, N. Y., November 8th, 1872; (3) Susan Wallace, born at Saratoga, N. Y., November 1st, 1873; (4 and 5) John Mason and Nathan Guilford, born at Philadelphia, Pa., January 2d, 1876.

The Braddock's Field estate, came by inheritance to George Wallace (2d), under the provisions of whose will it passed to his nephew, George Wallace (3d), shortly before his marriage, the widow having relinquished to him her life interest therein. The property was, however, entailed to the heirs male—first, of George Wallace (3d)— next, of his brother, James. If both died without male

GEORGE WALLACE.

From a portrait painted about 1840.

MARY WALLACE GUILFORD.

From a photograph taken in 1880.

children it was to go to their sister Martha and her heirs; and in case of her death to Jane and her heirs. James and Martha died unmarried. George, being without male heir and becoming involved in financial difficulties, conveyed his interest in the Braddock estate to the Bank of Pittsburgh, whose title to the fee of the property seems never to have been assailed. An important industrial town has since grown up on the spot.

During the last ten or fifteen years it has accidentally transpired that George Wallace was, at the time of his death, the recorded owner of landed property in Pittsburgh and Allegheny City, now become of considerable value, but lost to his heirs through long adverse possession and the operation of the statute of limitations.

MARY JANE WALLACE, second daughter of George Wallace, was born at Braddock Dec. 10th, 1841, and in 1865 married Nathan Guilford.

THE COOK FAMILY.

✤ ✤ ✤

GEORGE COOK, born in Holland, emigrated to America in the latter part of the eighteenth century with his wife, Susanna Cromley, and their two children, George and Mary. They settled in Philadelphia where he died. His wife, who survived him, died there in 1825. Their daughter Mary married ·Charles Lee, of Philadelphia, and had four children:

1. Susan, who married —— Hardy.
2. Mary, who married Horatio More.
3. Jane, who married Thomas Duane, and
4. William (unmarried).

GEORGE COOK, (2d), eldest child of George, was born in Holland in 1782 and died in Philadelphia in 1826. He married in 1806 Rachel Hoffman, who was born in New York in 1790 and died in Philadelphia in 1832. They had seven children, viz.:

1. John, born 1807, died (unmarried) 1825.
2. George, born 1808, died (unmarried) 1838.
3. Charles, born 1810, died 1852; married Martha Goff, of Philadelphia. His children were:

   (1) Martha, who married John Crossman; (2) George, born 1839, fatally wounded in 1862 at the battle of Fair Oaks; (3) Susan, died 1853.
4. Edward, born 1814, died unmarried.
5. Susanna.

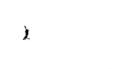

MARY WALLACE GUILFORD.

From a photograph taken in 1897.

SUSANNA COOK WALLACE.

From a photograph taken about 1890.

1

6. Jacob Wheeler, born 1819, died 1883, married Elvira McKowen. They had five children, viz

(1) Edward Simpson, died unmarried; (2) Elizabeth Rogers, married David B. Stewart; (3) George Adam, died unmarried; (4) Susanna Wallace, married Samuel D. Culbertson; (5) Thomas McK., married Clara Walton.

7. Mary Ann, born 1823, married John Singer, of Pittsburgh.

Rachael Hoffmann's father died in 1790, and his widow married Jacob Wheeler, of Philadelphia. The children of this marriage were:

1. Mary Wheeler, who married Jacob Paul, of Germantown, Pa. Their children were:

(1) Susan Paul, married William McCandless, of Pittsburgh; (2) Thaddeus Paul, married Phœbe Reamer; (3) Rachel Paul, married John Pears; (4) Jacob Paul, married Susan Fries (his cousin).

2. Ann Wheeler, who married Adam Fries. Their children were:

(1) Solomon Fries; (2) Christina Fries, married William Metcalf, of Pittsburgh; (3) Susan Fries, married Jacob Paul.

3. John Wheeler.
4. Jacob Wheeler.

SUSANNA COOK, daughter of George Cook, was born in Philadelphia Nov. 20th, 1818, and in 1835 married George Wallace.

GUILFORD
LINE OF DESCENT.

John Guilford, of Hingham, Mass.=Susanna, daughter of Wm. Norton, of Hingham

Susanna   Paul Guilford, of Hingham=Susanna Pullen   Priscill[a]

Mary   Elizabeth   Hester   William Guilford of Hingham, Scituate and Leicester

William Guilford=ane Thayer of Leicester and Williamsburg (See page 70 for descendants)

John Guilford, of Leicester=Susanna, daughter of Thomas Whitney, of Shrewsbury, Mass.

John   Asa   Samuel   Jonas Guilford=Lydia, daughter of John Hobbs, of Brookfield, Mass. of Spencer   William   Lucy   Nathan

Detsey   Nathan Guilford=Eliza W., daughter of Oliver Farnsworth of Newport, R. I. and Cincinnati. of Spencer, Mass. and Cincinnati, Ohio.   Jonas   Charles   John   Lydia   Sally   George   Asa

Anna   Elizabeth Donaldson   William   Apolline   Belle   Nathan Guilford=Mary J., daughter of Geo. Wallace, of Braddock's Field and Pittsburgh, Pa.

1	William B. 1848
2	Eugene L. 1850
3	Horace H. 1852
4	Charlotte 1854
5	Henry H. 1856
6	Charles W. 1858
7	Edwin B. 1867
8	May 1867
9	Nathan 1870

Clement Tétedoux
Marie Tétedoux

Minnie Stewart
Charles Barry
Florence Barry

Susan 1868   Nathan born 1867   Mary born 1872   Wallace born 1873.   Gertrude born 1880

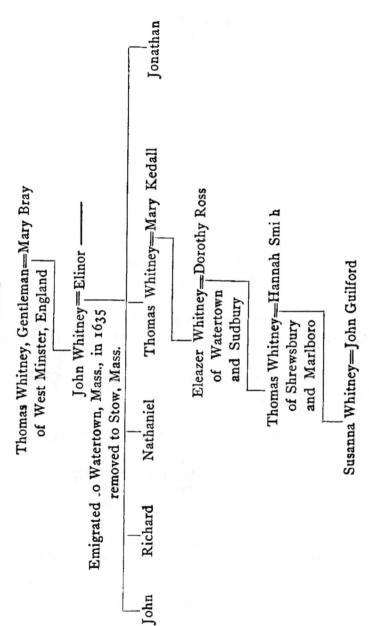

BROWNE
LINE OF DESCENT.

1. John Browne, of the borough of Stamford, County Lincoln, England. Alderman of Stamford in 1376 and 1377.

2. John Browne, of Stamford.

3. John Browne, of Stamford. Alderman 1414, 1422, 1427. Married Margery ——, died July 26th, 1442 ; was buried at All Saints' Church, erected at his expense.

4. John Browne, of Stamford. Alderman 1448, 1453, 1462. Married Agnes ——, who died 1470.

5. Christopher Browne, of Stamford and of Tolethorpe, County Rutland. Sheriff of Rutlandshire 1492–1500. Sided with Richmond against Richard III. Died 1518.

6. Christopher Browne, of Swan Hall, Parish of Hawkdon, County Suffolk. His will proved 1538. He married Anne ——.

7. Christopher Browne, of Swan Hall. Church-warden 1564; will proved 1594.

8. Thomas Browne, of Swan Hall; died 1590, married Joan ——

9. Abraham Browne, 5th son of Thomas, emigrated to Watertown, Mass., with wife Lydia and two children. Freeman 1631, selectman and land surveyor. Died 1650.

10. Jonathan Browne, born in Watertown October 15th, 1635, died 1691 ; married February 11th, 1661–2 Mary Shattuck (born 1645, died October 23d, 1732), daughter of Willian Shattuck (born 1621, settled in Watertown 1642, died August 14th, 1672), and his wife Susanna Shattuck (died December 11th, 1686).

11. Mary Browne, born October 5th, 1662, married Ensign John Warren.

FARNSWORTH

LINE OF DESCENT.

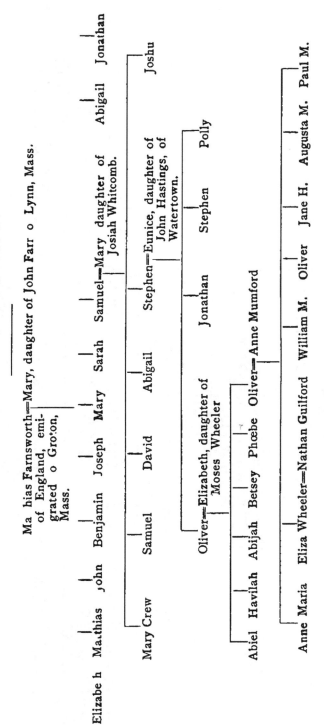

63

MUMFORD

LINE OF DESCENT.

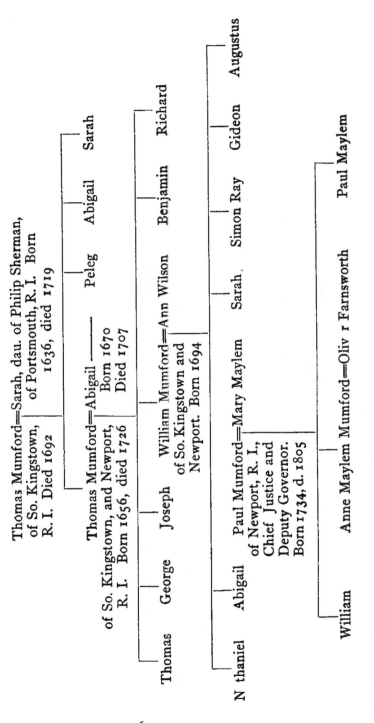

Thomas Mumford=Sarah, dau. of Philip Sherman,
of So. Kingstown,   of Portsmouth, R. I. Born
R. I. Died 1692   1636, died 1719

Thomas Mumford=Abigail ———   Peleg   Abigail   Sarah
of So. Kingstown, and Newport,   Born 1670
R. I. Born 1656, died 1726   Died 1707

William Mumford=Ann Wilson   Benjamin   Richard
of So. Kingstown and
Newport. Born 1694

Thomas   George   Joseph

Paul Mumford=Mary Maylem   Sarah.   Simon Ray   Gideon   Augustus
of Newport, R. I.,
Chief Justice and
Deputy Governor.
Born 1734, d. 1805

N thaniel   Abigail

Anne Maylem Mumford=Oliv r Farnsworth   Paul Maylem

William

SHERMAN

LINE OF DESCENT.

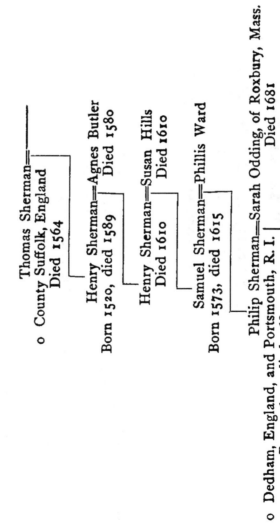

Thomas Sherman=
o County Suffolk, England
Died 1564

Henry Sherman=Agnes Butler
Born 1520, died 1589   Died 1580

Henry Sherman=Susan Hills
Died 1610   Died 1610

Samuel Sherman=Phillis Ward
Born 1573, died 1615

Philip Sherman=Sarah Odding, of Roxbury, Mass.
o Dedham, England, and Portsmouth, R. I.   Died 1681
Born 1610, died 1687

Sarah Sherman=Thomas Mumford
Born 1636, died 1719

WALLACE

LINE OF DESCENT

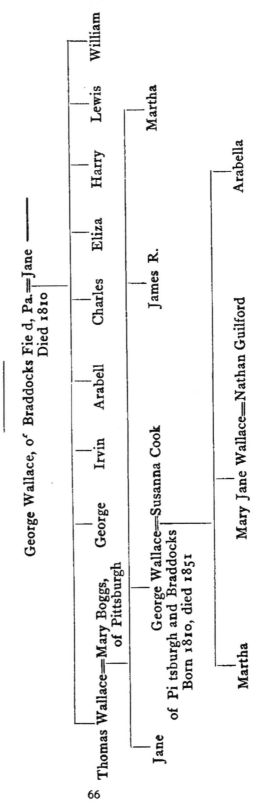

DESCENDANTS OF WILLIAM GUILFORD (2d)
OF LEICESTER, MASS.

❧ ❧ ❧

WILLIAM GUILFORD, son of William and brother of my great-grandfather John, married Jane Thayer, was a member of the Congregational Church in Leicester, and moved in 1750 to Williamsburg. He may have been the William Guilford who enlisted in 1747 in General Waldo's regiment in the old French and Indian War*. His children were:

1. Paul, born March 11th, 1740, who had two sons, Paul and Simeon.

2. Michael, born March 26th, 1742.

3. William, born September, 1744, who had two sons, Eleazer and John.

4. Noah, born May 23d, 1747.

5. Timothy, born September 10th, 1749, who married Betsey Hayden, and had three sons, Michael, Willard and George, and two daughters.

6. Simeon.

7. Hephzibah, born 1753, who married Paul Clapp.

SIMEON GUILFORD, sixth son of William, was born in November, 1751, and married Ruhannah Hayden. In March, 1776, he volunteered in the Massachusetts colonial service, and in December, 1777, he enlisted in the Continental army; he re-enlisted April, 1781, and in December, 1783, was discharged as Ensign, having served throughout the Revolutionary war. During his

*Knox MSS. Vol. xxvii, p. 418.

service he was at one time clerk to General Washington, and was present at the execution of the sentence of death on Major André. He lived to the age of 95 and had five children :

1. Esther, born June 22d, 1789, died February 9th, 1835; married Theophilus Packard.

2. Joshua, born February 19th, 1791; married (1) Mary Hodge, (2) Elizabeth Smith.

3. Electa, born March 19th, 1794, married Willard Gay.

4. Ruhannah, born October 31st, 1798, died October 20th, 1840; married Joseph Shepard Hayden.

5. Simeon.

SIMEON GUILFORD, youngest son of Simeon, was born near Northampton, Mass., May 10th, 1801. At the age of eighteen he was rodman in a corps of engineers locating the Erie Canal. In 1824 he went to Lebanon County, Pennsylvania, and was for some years engaged on the canals and public works of that State, holding for a time the office of chief engineer in the service of the State. He erected and operated the Swatara Furnace, and was one of the originators and operators of the Dudley Iron Co. of Lebanon. He died in Lebanon February 16th, 1895, aged 94 years. In May, 1830, he married Catharine Doll. Their children were :

1. A son, unnamed.

2. William Moore, born November 26th, 1832; married Mary Elder.

3. Mary Doll, born September 23d, 1834, died September 20th, 1870; married John Evans.

4. Robert Emmet, born March 18th, 1837, married ———— Hayden.

5. Simeon Hayden, born April 11th, 1841, married Virginia Gleim.

6. Charles Bingham, born June 25th, 1843, died July 12th, 1844.

Children of Dr. William Moore Guilford:

1. Catherine, born January 20th, 1858, died April 7th, 1862.
2. Simeon, born December 25th, 1859, died October 11th, 1870.
3. Jane, born February 12th, 1863, married John Hurst.
4. Mary, born September 12th, 1865, died June 30th, 1866.
5. William M., born February 16th, 1868.
6. Paul, born April 9th, 1870.
7. Adaline, born November 26th, 1872.
8. Arthur, born April 23d, 1880.

Children of Robert Emmet Guilford, of Shelbyville, Ill.

1. Kate.
2. Gertrude.
3. Simeon.

Children of Dr. Simeon Hayden Guilford, of Philadelphia.

1. Frank.
2. Elizabeth.
3. Dudley.
4. Charles.

LINE OF DESCENT
of the children of WILLIAM GUILFORD (2d,), of Leicester, Mass.

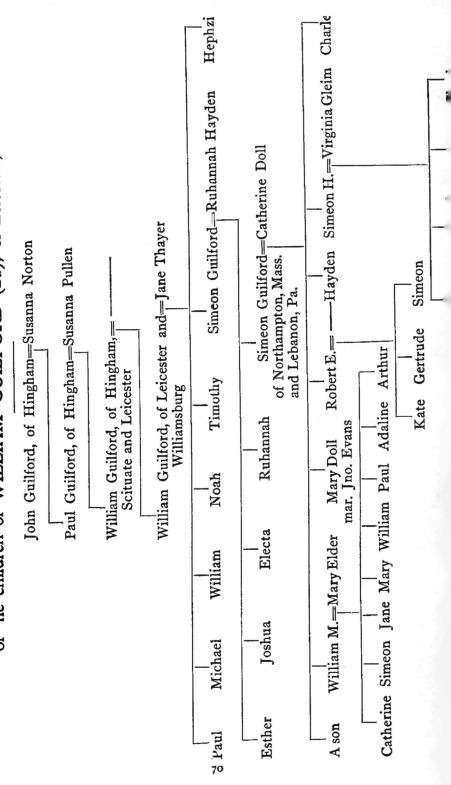

70

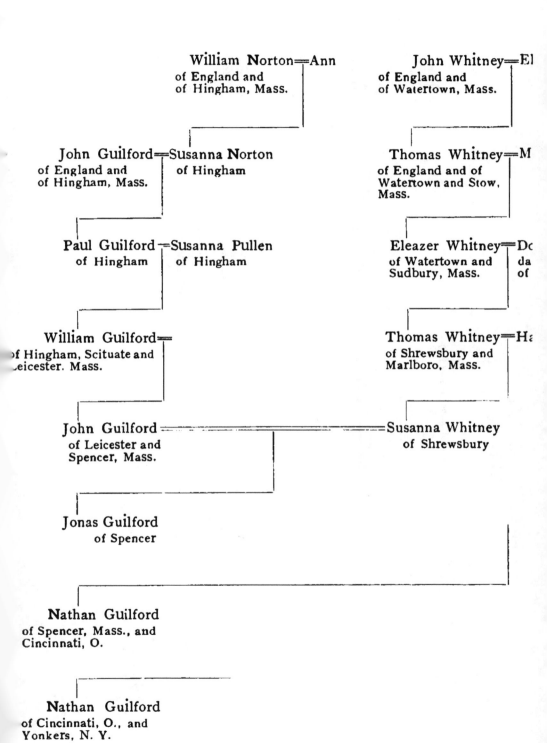

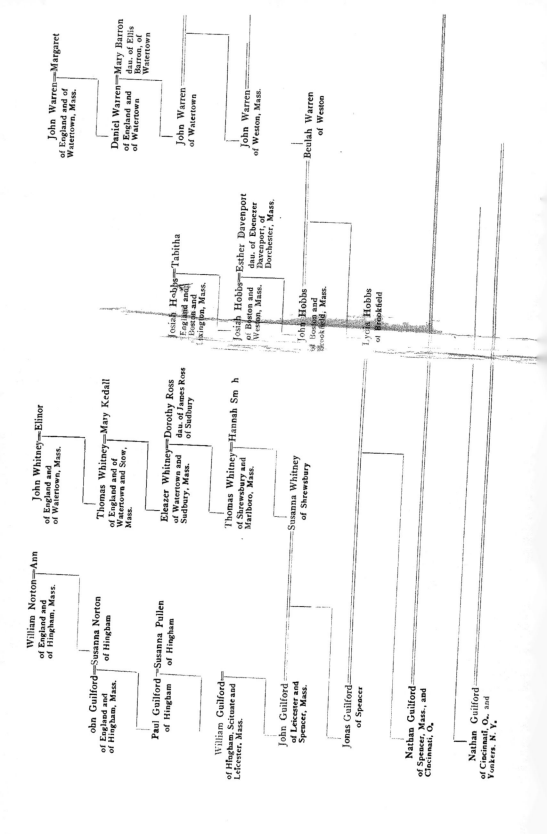

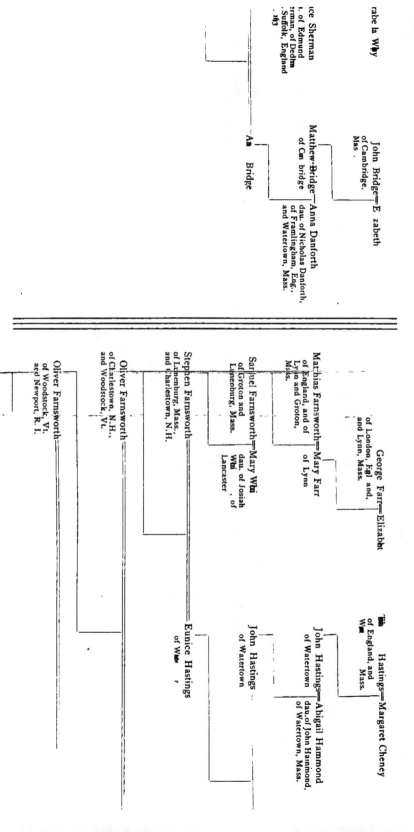

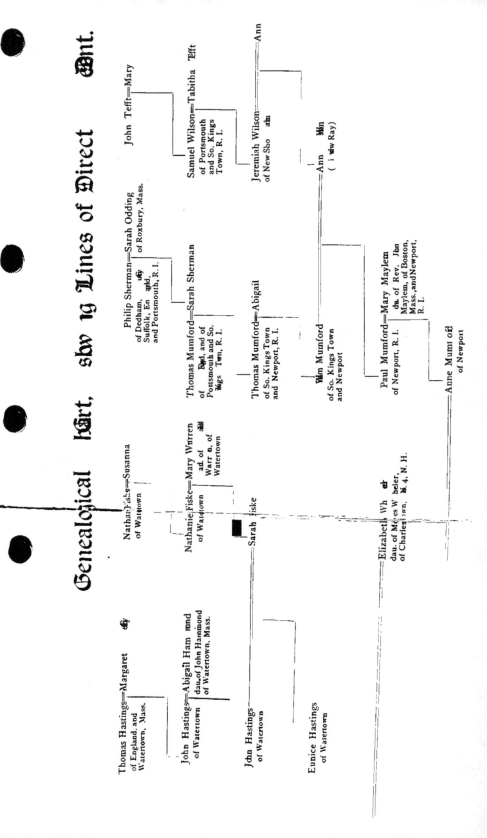

CPSIA information can be obtained
at www.ICGtesting.com
Printed in the USA
LVHW05s0351050818
585969LV00030B/317/P